Cognitive Therapy For Anxiety

How To Finally Break Free From Anxiety And Change Your Life Forever

By

Jonathan Moran

Table of Contents

Introduction

Being anxious can seem like a small problem, we all feel it at some point in our lives. Whether it is speaking in public or sitting an exam, anxiety is a natural process. For some, anxiety can ruin their lives. Experiencing a panic attack is not a pleasant experience. It can be debilitating and restrict your day to day life.

Yet, the process of anxiety is a biological one. As the body enters emergency mode, a release of hormones rush at the brain, which reacts with a fight or flight response. Imagine if you felt like this all the time and not only when threatened! This is what happens to those who suffer from anxiety. Their body is constantly on edge, expecting danger.

You are reading this book for a reason. You may simply be curious, or you may want to learn more about the healing process from anxiety attacks.

Help is at hand throughout these pages. It is important to understand what is happening to you as you face a draining panic attack. Only then can you begin to unravel the complexities of anxiety.

It is difficult to comprehend what a panic attack feels like unless you experience it firsthand. My own experiences cost me dearly. Gradually I withdrew from everyday life. I did anything to avoid that all too familiar feeling of dread. That's when my research began. Many years later I hold an MSc in Psychology, to substantiate my theories.

Now is the time to take back control of your inner self. To stave off future panic attacks, you should learn how your body reacts and how to take control. You can influence, to some extent, your hormonal release. This will stop those attacks right in their tracks. Amazingly, it is not a difficult task to take on. Once you do, your life will improve and you will gain the freedom to go anywhere at any time. It is liberating for those living under the sentence of anxiety.

Cognitive Behavior therapy (CBT) is a way of curing many mental health issues. It has a proven track record on conditions such as PTSD and GAD. For those reasons, CBT is one of the most widely used therapies for such conditions. There are various methods, all giving excellent results. Seeking professional help may entail individual or group therapy for 5-20 weeks in a clinic setting. Or you can look at self-help, using similar techniques.

By learning to identify the warning signals, you will learn to control future anxiety episodes. Simple relaxation exercises help you control the hormonal levels occurring in your body. CBT shows you how to change thought patterns so depression and panic are kept at bay.

When writing this book, it was my intention to show you how easy it is to change your life around. This is something you can begin today, not tomorrow or next week. Start the CBT sessions now! The sooner you start, the sooner you get your life back under control.

Do you suffer dark thoughts? CBT will help you change such thoughts around completely. Our inner emotions are the true grit of who we are. It stands to reason that if we connect with them we can balance our mental health processes.

Don't allow your self-esteem to plunge into the dark pits of insecurity, as your negative thinking takes over. Read on to find your secret inner powers, where CBT can help you lead a confident and normal life.

Chapter 1 Overview of CBT and why it works

Pioneering Therapy

Aaron Beck's pioneering work in psychotherapy led to the introduction of Cognitive Behavior therapy (CBT). He was an American Psychologist and professor at the University of Pennsylvania.

CBT has similarities to psychotherapy. Both relate to the treatment and possible cure for mental health conditions. CBT concentrates on thoughts, attitudes and beliefs and how these affect a person's behavior. It is based on the premise that how a person feels, acts and thinks, are all interconnected. If any one of these factors can be altered, then they can all be changed. This type of therapy targets the negative thought patterns that have led to the cycle of distorted behavior. It is a theory also known as Negative Reinforcement.

The understanding that thoughts can shape how a person feels and behave, is not a new concept. The Greek philosopher Epictetus said, *People are not disturbed by things, but by the view they take of them.* This is the basis of CBT. It is not the situations that cause people to suffer mental health problems, but rather their own interpretation of them.

Therapists who work with CBT play more of a supervisory role, rather than a consultant. Their role is to oversee the client's personal development and ensure their wellbeing.

Emotional Reasoning

A major cause of mental health problems can be Emotional Reasoning. This refers to allowing emotions to determine thoughts.

For example, believing that

something must be true because
we feel it is.

This can and does affect how people relate to the world.

For example, if you pass an
acquaintance on the street and
they do not respond to your
greeting. Your reaction and
thought pattern could be that
you believe they do not like you.
Though you don't know this for
sure, but now you feel rejected.
In turn, your thoughts further
spiral into other negative
aspects of yourself. If this was
to happen on a regular basis,
then your opinion of yourself is
lowered. With low self-esteem
comes depression and anxiety.

Cognitive Distortions

CBT attempts to challenge negative thought patterns. When they are identified, they will be replaced with positive thoughts. It attempts to identify common negative thinking styles, known as Cognitive Distortions, such as:

- Emotional Reasoning - I feel useless, therefore I am.
- Jumping to conclusions - That person ignored me today, they must dislike me.
- All or Nothing - Everything is Black and white, with no grey areas in-between. This can also be known as Labeling.
- Filtering - Giving prominence to your own failures rather than your successes. This is because the sufferer does not identify any successes.
- Overgeneralization - Thought patterns determine future outcomes.

For example, the failure to get a job after an interview could lead to Overgeneralization. The result of their experience distorts their thinking pattern, and they now believe that they will never get a job.

These are only a few standards of Cognitive Distortions that can lead to mental health issues, such as depression and anxiety.

CBT attempts to tackle Cognitive Distortions by teaching the patient more positive ways of thinking. There are a few strategies to do this, but it usually begins with Functional Analysis. This means first identifying the negative thought patterns of the client. 'The therapist will then determine the behaviors that go with the Cognitive Distortion. With the goals in mind, the therapist will attempt to teach the patient new skills to overcome the negative thinking.

CBT is recognized as being useful for treating many mental health illnesses, such as:

- Depression
- Anxiety
- Addictions
- Phobias
- Eating disorders.

Text In the western world, the gold standard of counseling is seen as the best, defined by evidence in its success. CBT is one such therapy that falls into this status of "gold standard." Most patients suffering from mental health issues are referred for CBT treatment. It has many benefits over using medication as a treatment. As a stand-alone treatment, it also has fewer side effects than drugs. Often though, it can be combined with drug therapy.

How CBT therapy works

The primary goal of CBT is to tackle the negative thinking patterns that are the root cause of so many issues. It differs from other methods of psychoanalysis that tend to be more freestyle. They are often based on self-exploration, by using a set structure for their methods. There is still some self-exploration involved in CBT. Patients are encouraged to analyze their inner-feelings and more importantly, their deep thoughts. Sometimes the therapist may set homework for the patient to do alone. The following techniques can involve a worksheet for the patient to follow:

- Self-Journals - keeping a diary about their thoughts and emotions. Most especially when linked to events that may cause them problematic issues. This can be a good way to identify trigger points of certain emotions.

- Breaking down the Cognitive Distortions - seen as the main goal of CBT. Identifying

14

harmful thoughts is the first step in learning how to control them.

- Cognitive rebalancing - this leads on to the next phase. Once the distortions are identified, it is then possible to find the root cause of those distortions. With help from a CBT counselor, the patient can then begin to understand why they feel the way they do. This is especially helpful if the patient's thoughts are harmful. It is an important step in helping them to challenge their thoughts.

- Interoceptive Exposure - also known as Gradual Exposure. A technique used to help treat panic attacks. Panic attacks often happen as a response to sensations in the body, such as shudders, tingling or even nausea. Interoceptive Exposure exposes the client to the feelings that bring on such sensations. The patient is guided to see that their thoughts are maladaptive or abnormal. They learn that i is the dysfunctional thinking that results in triggering a panic attack. They are encouraged to confront such thoughts and not avoid them. Only then can they recognize that the resulting sensations that come with the thoughts are not a threat. This method is also used to treat Obsessive Compulsive Disorder (OCD), and those who suffer from phobias.

- Progressive Muscle Relaxation - this uses relaxation exercises and is a similar technique to mindfulness. The exercises involve relaxing one muscle group at a time, until total relaxation of the body is achieved. Grossman et al (2004)(1a), carried out a meta-analysis of previous studies on this technique. He indicates that mindfulness can help with stress and anxiety. Breathing techniques are also used to help the patient achieve a state of relaxation.

- Functional Analysis - is a means of identifying the event that causes the cognitive distortions and behavior initially. In short, cause-effect-consequences. This method is usually accompanied by a worksheet. It allows the patient to make notes on the episode that causes the dysfunctional thoughts. They must record the behavior those thoughts instigated, and any consequences that followed.

There are a multitude of other techniques, or skills, which the supervisor can use in a CBT session. Far too many for the scope of this book. In understanding some of the techniques, it shows how this therapy can work.

Whilst there are many different skill sets in a CBT therapist's armory, there are also a few therapeutic approaches they can use.

- Cognitive Therapy - is the standard CBT approach. This method which looks at maladaptive/dysfunctional thoughts and how to change them

- Dialectical Behavioural Therapy (DBT) - an approach that was originally used to treat borderline personality disorder (BPD.) It was also found to be effective in treating a much wider range of issues. For Instance, eating disorders, substance abuse, bipolar, as well as many others.

- Multi-modal Therapy (MMD) - is an eclectic therapy that draws from other psychotherapies. MMD has a basis that there are seven different aspects to psychological functioning, known as the Basic ID. These are first assessed before treatment continues.

- Rational Emotive Behaviour Therapy (REBT) - an approach that can be used to help patients change irrational beliefs.

Does CBT Therapy work?

Among the non-pharmacutical remedies, CBT has the most clinical evidence to show its success. Studies show that it is at least as effective as using psychotropic drugs, for anxiety and depression and bipolar, Chang et al (2017) (1b). Usually, CBT is a short-term treatment, often lasting for less than six months. Once the patient has developed new ways of thinking and how to challenge maladaptive thoughts, then over time they still benefit from CBT.

One reason this therapy is deemed effective is how the brain reacts to CBT. In an event such as an anxiety or a panic attack, certain areas of the brain are overreacting. These areas are known as the amygdala. It regulates emotions and the hippocampus which processes memory. Using brain scans on those who have anxiety issues, have shown that such brain regions return to normal levels of activity after CBT. Beutel et al (2010) (1c).

Chapter 2 Understanding anxiety and the anxious mind

Historical Treatment of Anxiety

The World Health Organization (WHO), reported that 300 million people worldwide suffer from depression. That is almost 1/5th of the world's population. Depression is also believed to be the No.1 contributing disability in the world. Anxiety disorders ranked at 6th. These statistics make sad reading. The US has one of the highest rates of anxiety. With 8 people in every 100, suffering anxiety disorders in some form WHO (2017).

Studies are also showing that common mental health disorders occur at a higher rate in the lower income sectors. Even more disturbing is the fact that anxiety disorders are treatable. Why then are the figures so high? Is it a modern epidemic?

In medieval times treatment consisted of blood leaches and bathing in freezing water. It was a real breakthrough when psychologists such as Sigmund Freud, started treating sufferers more as patients. Such patients began to undergo the "talking" therapy. It was not until as late as the 1980's that the American Psychiatric Association recognized "anxiety" as a mental health disorder. Before then, anxiety was simply classed as a "woman's problem." Sufferers became stigmatized and labeled as depressives. Women are twice as likely to suffer from anxiety disorders, but such conditions are by no means restricted to females only. Today, anxiety may be treated with medication as well as therapy.

What is Anxiety?

In days gone by, our ancestors risked their lives whenever they hunted live food. Luckily, these skills are no longer needed, but it brings us to how the body reacts when facing danger. This is a time when we instinctively make the decision of "fight, flight or freeze." It's not a choice brought on by conscious thought. Rather, it is set in motion by the release of chemicals in the part of our brain known as the limbic system. The chemical is cortisol, which is a steroid hormone released through the adrenalin glands. One of the side effects from raised levels of this hormone is anxiety. If you feel this type of anxiety too often, the high levels of cortisol can damage cells in a part of the brain known as the hippocampus. This is an area that helps process memories. Such damage can lead to impaired learning and loss of memory. McAuley et all (2009)(2a). de Quervain et al (1998) (2b).

Symptoms of Anxiety

Anxiety is now separated from the condition of depression. Although many who suffer from depression also have anxiety issues. Patients who suffer from depression tend to dwell on the past and feel very negative about themselves, and life in general. This is not typical in the case of patients suffering from anxiety. They will worry excessively about the here and now, or the future. Their lives are full of "what ifs," in the eventuality of a disaster. Symptoms of anxiety can vary in individuals, but here are a few to look out for:

- Feeling tense for no reason, on edge and almost nervous.
- The sense of dread and impending doom.
- Unable to sleep because of worry.
- General restlessness and fidgeting, unable to relax.
- Lack of concentration.
- Irritable for no reason.
- Breaking out in a cold sweat.
- Shaking.
- Feeling nauseous.
- Digestive and intestinal upsets.

Panic attacks can come as a result of feeling one or many of these symptoms. When someone has frequent anxiety attacks, it inevitably leads to ill health. This is because of the cortisol levels remain high too often and for too long. One of cortisol's roles is to increase blood sugars. Unbalanced and this can result in insulin resistance. In turn, this may lead to the late onset or type 2 diabetes. Hacket et al (2016) (2c).

In a modern fast-paced society with access to social media, many people are feeling more and more anxious about the world around us. This can start at an early age. If young people are not diagnosed and treated, their anxiety attacks will follow them into adulthood.

There are also various stages throughout life that can lead to feeling over anxious:

- Education

Learning and education should be an enjoyable experience. All too often children are pressured to meet certain academic targets. Those who don't meet them may very well consider themselves a failure. The burden of being successful lays heavy on the shoulders of young people.

- Family life.

This is a worrying time, particularly if you have never had responsibilities. Women are expected to raise families and go out to work at the same time. Such pressures create huge stresses in their daily lives. With the increasing break up of marriages, the pressure of anxiety reflects on both parents, and on the children.

- Materialism

People who live in wealthy industrialized countries are bombarded with a heavily commercialized culture. Advertising constantly prompts us to buy the newest and seemingly greatest ever products. Such deviant tactics imply that their goods will improve your life and make you happy. It seems we must keep up with all the latest gadgets to have an attractive home, and wear the latest fashion labels to look good. All increasing the pressures of life as we attempt to earn more money to keep up.

- The Anxious Mind

Whilst it might seem to be stating the obvious, worry plays a key role in anxiety. People who suffer from anxiety attacks are likely big worriers. Often, the only way a worrier will stop panicking over a specific problem is if they have moved on to a different one. Worry leads to anxiety until the released chemicals mean the person cannot think rationally. At this point, they will jump to conclusions of their own making. Unable to focus on reality because their minds are highly aroused, the problem is no longer solvable. They cannot see any solutions which then leads deeper into anxiety.

- Simple Coping Techniques

For those who experience the build-up of burdening pressures and suffer anxiety attacks, there is help available. We will look at this in more detail later in this book. There are lifestyle changes that can be put into practice, using techniques to nip the anxiety attacks in the bud. A sufferer may find that these techniques are all they need to alleviate the experience of anxiety. Such as:

- Discussing your anxiety issues with your doctor. Doctors can prescribe medication to help you initially, and then refer you to a CBT therapist.

- Look at the foods you eat and what you drink. Caffeine and alcohol can both effect anxiety levels negatively. Take the general advice and at the very least cut down on the intake of foods known to cause such effects.

- Exercise is beneficial, but it doesn't mean you must work-out like crazy at a gym. Go on walks in calm and soothing vistas, if possible. Learn relaxation exercises that you can do sitting at a desk or watching TV, such breathing exercises and muscle relaxation.

- Try and keep active so you tire yourself out naturally during the day. That way sleep will come easier at night.

Stress and anxiety are closely related conditions. Though it is possible to suffer one without suffering the other. For both, you should seek help but there are many self-help techniques that you can do to ease some of the immediate pressures.

Anxiety can include phobias and is often only triggered in certain circumstances. Stress is more a build-up of worry because there is too much pressure in your life. Something has to give. We will look at ways of helping yourself to cope with anxiety. Many of the coping methods are ways to ease the pressures, are similar to the stress self-help approach. It could be that stress is what has brought on your anxiety in the first place. Deal with one and the other may ease as well.

Recognizing that you are suffering from anxiety is the first stage. Events such as employment interviews will naturally cause anxious feelings, these are normal. You should not worry about anxiety when associated with common stressful events. Having adrenalin coursing through your system when under such stress, is a way your body copes with the situation. When you come out of the interview, the anxiety should lift to be replaced with relief that the stress is over. Of course, you may then stress while you wait for the results but try not to be over anxious in such situations.

It is when you are anxious over too many things, especially every day and maybe even all day. This is unhealthy as you will be producing those hormones we mentioned earlier, in high amounts. If you find that stress is affecting your everyday life, then it is time to seek help. The stress will mount up causing triggers to anxiety attacks. Hopefully, you will recognize the dire situation before it gets to that point.

If you have suffered anxiety attacks for over 6 months, this is known as Generalized Anxiety Disorder (GAD). Our next chapter will help you to assess yourself and recognize if this is you.

Chapter 3 Developing your anxiety profile

Matching Anxiety Types with Anxiety Programs

Quote: Natalie Goldberg Author who believes in and explores Zen Buddhism. "Stress is an ignorant state. It believes that everything is an emergency."

Self-diagnosis is not encouraged when it comes to health issues, but anxiety can be eased with self-control. To do this, you will need to think about "when, where and what" triggers your own symptoms. Because there are various types of anxiety, it could be helpful to recognize which one you are suffering from. Learning the various types of anxiety and seeking the correct treatment for it, is important in the process of self-help. We will go into detailed treatment options later in this book. This chapter will look at ways you can identify your anxiety type and outline possible options for self-help treatment.

Let's start with some of the more serious profiles for the onset of anxiety. Post-Traumatic Stress Disorder (PTSD) is not as prevalent as generalized anxiety. The rarer types are usually brought on from specific events. By learning the various anxiety types, it will help you categorize your own anxiety profile. Once you understand your own profile, you will be better able to know which treatments might help you.

PTSD

Situation:

This relates to people who have experienced a traumatic incident that is out of the ordinary. It is usually an event that is not considered the norm, such as:

- Soldiers in combat.

- Childhood abuse.

- Rape or physical attack.

- Witnessing a murder.

- Natural disasters.

This list is only an example, but it shows the unusual circumstances that someone suffering PTSD may have gone through.

Symptoms:

They will suffer symptoms such as:

- Reliving the experience as if in a daydream. The event will play out in their minds with a feeling that the experience is happening right here and now.
- Reliving the experience in a nightmare when they sleep.
- Bad dreams will lead to broken sleep.
- Broken sleepwalk lead to irritability.

- Trigger points can set off the memory and lead to a panic attack.
- They may begin to avoid places and people. This is because they become frightened of any reminders of the traumatic event.
- Anger issues can set in as they are always on guard.
- Sufferers may become easily startled and have difficulties concentrating.

PTSD sufferers may find their minds focusing on the traumatic memories more and more each day. This can lead to the inability to cope with the normality around them. Sadly, they may try to forget by taking drugs or alcohol.

The onset of PTSD symptoms can be delayed by months or even years after their experiences. It can be a gradual process before the patient finally breaks down. Anxiety symptoms may not be diagnosed until it comes in the form of panic attacks. It is likely that they will suffer the symptoms of depression first. PTSD does not only effect victims of traumatic incidents, it can include anyone who witnesses such an event.

Treatment:

Self-help alone cannot treat the symptoms someone with PTSD will suffer. Only when a PTSD patient can control their maladaptive thought process, can they begin their self-help process

- Medication can be an important first step and a valuable tool in the beginning of their treatment.
- Attending group sessions with other PTSD suffers can help them to talk about their experiences. Support groups will consist of fellow sufferers, so the patient can see that they are not alone.
- Family counseling can be helpful to allow those closest to them to understand what they are going through. This also helps families to

realize their loved one is suffering an illness. Then they too can provide that all important support.

Phobias

This is when a person feels afraid of a particular sight, smell or situation.

Situation:

- It could come in the form of seeing insects, blood or even certain smells.
- Or it could come from an experience of heights or being enclosed in an elevator.

Symptoms:

- When in that situation, they begin to imagine extreme consequences; What if I fall and die and nobody finds me? What if the spiders go inside my body? What if the elevator gets stuck and no one knows?

- Feelings will be a sense of dread, shallow breathing, dizziness, cold sweats, nausea.
- It can bring on a panic attack.
- They will begin to avoid any situation that might entail such fears. Someone with a fear of spiders may no longer enjoy working in a garden, even though they loved to before their phobia took hold.

Treatment:

- It may be a combination of self-help exercises similar to stopping a panic attack.
- Plus, there will be an element of exposure therapy which we cover in another chapter.

OCD

Situation:

- Someone suffering from OCD may have spent many years with generalized stress and anxiety.

- They may have suffered a terrible experience that brought on their anxieties in the first instance.
- It could be a build-up of many situations as to why an OCD sufferer becomes obsessed.

Symptoms:

- Everything around them is exaggerated and distressing in their minds.
- They feel that the world around them is intruding upon them all the time. To overcome this, they may pray over and over or repeat certain words of comfort to themselves.
- Other forms of OCD can lead to obsessive cleanliness and everything must be orderly.
- One OCD symptom is that of hoarding, in case they need it later.
- They will probably be aware of their irrational behavior, but cannot stop.
- Some have intrusive and disturbing thoughts. Thoughts such as, if I don't spin around to the

left 3 times, then someone in my family might come to harm. Or they may imagine they will get a disease if their home is not clean and tidy.

- For some, everything must be placed in a particular order.
- For others, they must carry out their rituals in a certain order.
- OCD is how they relieve their anxieties.

When it takes an extended time to complete rituals, it can take over their lives and become debilitating.

Treatment:

- Medication may be an option.
- Support from family members will be encouraged.
- Group therapy means sharing their worries and admitting their obsessive behavior.
- Exposure therapy is a good option for those who avoid certain situations. Learning to

confront their fear and seeing that all is still well in the world.

As with most anxiety conditions, it is all about gaining control again.

Panic Attacks

Situation:

This type of profile is more one of sudden intense fear.

- A sufferer may, or may not, know the reason for the reason for the onset of sheer fear.
- It is almost always a reaction to a bodily sensation, such as increased heartbeat or tightness in the chest.
- Symptoms:
- Heavy and fast breathing.
- This can lead on to a tingling sensation.

- Dry mouth causing and you may have difficulty swallowing, or even feel like they are choking.
- Hot and cold sweats.
- Light headedness and dizziness, believing they might collapse.
- Impending doom that something bad is about to happen.
- Imagining terrible scenarios, such as:
  - "I'm going to die."
  - "Someone is going to attack me, I don't feel safe."
  - "There's going to be a disaster and I won't be able to get away.
  - "I've lost all control."

The sufferer has started to feel anxious for some reason, and it has led on to a full-blown panic attack.

For example: You are sat in your car on

*the freeway in a huge traffic jam.
Normally you're patient in such
situations, but you have a meeting to
get to. Already the stress is setting in
because you have no control over the
situation. Then, you hear a car backfire
and it triggers off an anxious thought.
You start thinking, "What if someone's
running lose with a gun and we all think
it's just a car backfiring?" Now you
won't get out of the car because you're
imagining bad things. This makes you
feel trapped so your anxious thoughts
take control of you. You can't breathe
and you're all alone in the car. You start
to imagine that you're going to have a
heart attack. You start to breath quick
and shallow breaths, which leads onto
a tingling in your fingers. That's it, now
you know that today you are going to
die. All the signs are right. You are now
in a full-blown panic attack.*

Can you see how this happened?

- Clearly, this person is already suffering stress.
- They must get to the important meeting on time.
- Frustration is setting in as the delay increases their stress levels.
- This could play out in many ways. Perhaps, in the same scenario, the driver gets out of the vehicle and starts shouting and swearing at no one in particular. Then, if someone responds, the driver abuses them as they have now become the focus of their target.

The entire scenario has been caused by stress.

- Do you recognize any of these feelings happening to you, whereby you blow a situation out of proportion?
- See how easy stress can lead to feeling anxious, which can bring on a full-blown panic attack?

Treatment:

- Self-help treatment will be learning how to recognize and deal with the symptoms before they blow out of proportion.
- It may also involve medication initially, to help with relaxation.
- Learning simple relaxation exercises, such as mindfulness and deep breathing.

Generalized Anxiety

Situation:

We have looked at many anxiety conditions. Yet, being over-anxious can happen to anyone who is overloaded with stress. The main problem with generalized anxiety is that it never goes away. Everyone has everyday worries to contend with.

Symptoms:

- The first signs you are not coping is when you are constantly worrying until the worry is on your mind all the time.
- It will be a build-up to lots of small worries, such as will you get somewhere on time? Who's doing the school run? How can you pay bills?
- You may find yourself not eating breakfast because you woke up worrying.
- Suffering constipation because your body is to tense.
- Constant headaches.
- The situation escalates until you feel physically ill.

Treatment:

- Recognize that you are suffering anxiety.
- Self-help treatment begins with mindfulness. Recognizing; Acceptance; Setting out a plan of action to ease the stresses in your daily life.

Chapter 4 Seven practical CBT skills to practice

Improve condition and functioning to transform an anxious mind

The cycle of an anxiety attack is based on a trigger, usually a physical sensation, that leads to negative thoughts. Our imagination then runs wild. A roller coaster of mixed emotions result in our response and behavior. Yet, we as individuals with agency can learn to exert some control over this process. Self-help is an excellent option for the pathway of eliminating anxiety. As with any self-motivational task, practice leads to greater control.

There are many approaches to CBT therapy. Let's look at seven of them, to see how different CBT therapeutic methods can heal an anxious mind.

1. Journals and Data Gathering

When you are suffering from a constant barrage of

negative thoughts, it can be a very disturbing experience. It is not always easy to control the thoughts in your head. Particularly so when you are on a downward spiral of emotions. This is a time when need to learn exactly who your inner self really is.

Inner mind-talk

Do you ever talk to yourself? We can do this silently in our minds, or even out loud if you feel comfortable enough to do so. Don't worry or feel embarrassed, we all do it. It is when you do not realize that you are talking to yourself that it may become a mental health concern. If you catch yourself doing it, then you know all's well. Your inner self is attempting to organize and take control. Studies have shown that it is good to converse with yourself. One study indicates that when we talk out loud to ourselves, it actually boosts concentration. This, in turn, helps us to achieve our goals with the task in hand. (Kirkham, Breeze & Mari-Beffa (2011) (4.1a)

As you worry over a problem, your mind is gathering information to think up solutions. It could be described as data gathering if we were computers. As we're human though, it can be very distracting when your mind will not shut down.

Sometimes our mind-talk can be unhelpful. Especially if the thoughts are negative, and/or coming at us at inappropriate times. It can drive you to distraction. For instance at 2 am in the morning when you keep telling yourself to "go to sleep," and all your mind wants to do is worry. Later we will discuss breathing techniques for such relaxation. If this fails then don't lay there suffering, get up and read a book, listen to music, go get a drink of water. Any activity that may help to redirect your inner thoughts away from the constant state of worry.

You need to learn to deal with those worrying thoughts in a different way. Stop your mind from running away with inner thoughts at inappropriate times. There is a technique that will identify negative thoughts that keep re-occurring in your mind and redirect them. You will be digging into the mental noise that you may not even be aware of. You will achieve this by creating a journal of things that happen to you. In this journal, you will be encouraged to record the event and your feelings at the time. Later you will study the recordings and find solutions.

For example:

John is rushing to catch a bus to return home after his working day. It's the bus he gets at the same time every day. As he approaches the bus stop he can see who is waiting, and he stops rushing. He begins to think that maybe he'll let the bus go and catch the next one, even though it hasn't even arrived yet. Why is he suddenly afraid of catching a bus that he had been rushing to get?

It is not being on a bus that he is anxieties about. It is the people at the bus stop. They are fellow work colleagues and they are sat chatting and laughing. He's panicking as he is not a very popular person. He wonders should he talk to them and risk them ignoring him? Or should he ignore them and risk them thinking him unsocial? His mind is ticking over fast. Every thought becomes more negative, even to the point that he decides to go home using a different route. Only moments before he was in a good mood looking forward to catching the bus to get home. Now he wants to avoid the bus altogether and he'll get home later.

The result could be that John will have to

go out of his way to go home a different
way. This may lead on to other problems
such as leaving work later, when his work
colleagues have gone. John has resolved
nothing, only made his life harder.

In reality, all he needed to do was smile at one person in the group and respond if necessary. Instead, one negative thought led to another and the whole situation became unbearable for him.

Let's suppose that when John gets home, he writes the incident down in a journal. He would be encouraged to dissect the situation more slowly. It is an opportunity to review every thought and feeling he had in those speedy moments of panic. It is a way at pulling out your inner thoughts. Asking yourself questions about what you have written. Looking at other ways of how you "could" have dealt with the situation. This is a proven way of taking your time to assess what you perceived to be an anxious situation.

Writing a daily journal of your movements and feelings to study later, will give you an idea of your triggers. Use headings, such as "event," "emotion," "notes." You don't need to write down everything you do in a day, only the stressful situations.

What you need to do is focus on recording any flashes of anxiety, as John did in the example. Later that day, you can read what you were thinking at the time, pulling out on important key points. When John reads his diary log about his experience at the bus stop, he may see that it would not have been that difficult to get his usual bus. By seeing the truth of the situation, he will not change his route home. Instead, he will simply smile at those he knows. That is enough social grace to acknowledge their presence without too much input from him. If they don't respond, then at least he has not made a fool of himself. Already he has achieved a goal;

confronting people he doesn't feel comfortable with and refusing to go home a different way.

Worksheet Ideas

Daily Activity Diary

- This is about logging your activity during the day. At the end of the week, or in a therapy session, you then reflect upon your diary to help you evaluate your thoughts and actions.
- Workload It's not necessary to complete every session, every day if very little is happening.
- Activity. These are actives that brought about emotional responses. You don't need to write about the mundane tasks, such as cleaning your home. It is more important to focus on events that may cause you anxiety or fluctuations in your mood swing.
- Thoughts. When you write something in the Activity section, then you need to fill in the rest of the columns. In this section, it's so you

know whether your thoughts were negative or not.

- Mood. Here you should grade your mood between 1-10 at the time of the event. When you study the diary later, it will show you what makes you panic and what makes you moody.

- Answer problems. Try to think of ways to deal with the events that you are logging. Look at what you went wrong and write how you could have stopped it, or done things differently. You can put these answers in at the end of the day, or the end of the week when you come to studying your diary. if you do it later then you will not feel as emotional as when the event happened.

- Replacement Statement. This part is about counteracting any negative thoughts you had during the day. Pick out the parts of your day where you achieved something, no matter how trivial. Write about your day in a positive light.

Time	Activity	Thoughts	Mood 1= Great 10= Depressed	Answer to any problems
6 – 8 am	Stayed in bed	Don't want to get the train to work.	8-Tired	Should get up earlier.
8 - 10 am	Missed Brkfst, in a rush.	Caused myself to get stressed. Hate rushing	9-Panic I'll be late to work.	Set 2 alarms to get up earlier.
10am – 12noon	Ate unhealthy lunch as hungry.	Hate my job	7-Dreading journey home.	Get a job nearer home.
12 - 2pm	Supervisor gave me a telling off as I did some wrong inputting.	She's always had it in for me!	10-Angry.	I should get a new job.
2 - 4pm		I know it was my fault not my supervisors.	5	Stop worrying about journey home.
4 - 6pm	Train packed.	Should I sit here and wait for crowd to go.	10-Panickin!	I must stop doing that journey.

6 - 8pm	Finally got home.	Relieved to be home. I hate my life!	10-Crying.	Need to buy a car.
8 - 10pm	Go to bed early.	I like my job really. It's just the journey.	6-Fed up.	Save up for a car.
10pm – 12mdn t	Asleep for 10			

Replacement Statement: *Today I went to work even though I didn't want to go. I got on a train with lots of people which means that I am a brave person. My boss told me off but I deserved it as I did something wrong. I need a car but can't afford one, Instead, I'm going to be an early riser. I will defeat this problem by getting an earlier train that isn't so busy.*

Add new columns that are relevant to your own personal situation, if you wish to add more detail.

Note that the replacement statement is for you to change around the negative aspects of your day. Remind yourself of what you have achieved. In our example the client DID get to work, despite sleeping in. They DID get on the busy train, despite hating crowds. They DID take the criticism from their boss and admitted it was their own fault.

The idea behind these worksheets is for you and your therapist to study how you're behaving and thinking during a normal week. Then to analyze it and find solutions to many issues.

2. Cognitive Restructuring

This type of therapy is fundamental to CBT. It is also known as Cognitive Reframing. The idea behind it is to analyze negative thoughts and give them a whole new meaning. In this way, you are challenging those maladaptive thoughts.

Stress-producing thoughts are called Cognitive Distortions. Such a negative mindset affects your inner mood, making you unhappy and causing anxiety. With Cognitive Reframing the goal is to challenge Cognitive Distortions. To do this you will replace them with more positive cognitions and so reduce stress.

When a negative thought occurs due to a trigger, it can send you on a downward spiral of depression. This increases stress levels and ruins the quality of your life. Once in a negative mood swing, performance is affected. and you will find yourself becoming anxious at the most innocuous of situations. If you can learn to turn this around, then you will have much better control of your inner thoughts.

The process of Cognitive Restructuring was developed in the 1950's by psychologist, Albert Ellis. It was part of his development of Rational Emotive Behavior Therapy (REBT). It is successful in helping to treat many nervous disorders. Bryant et al (2006) carried out a study of this for PTSD sufferers(4.2a). The results indicated that Cognitive

Restructuring was effective in reducing depression and maladaptive thinking in PTSD patients. It is not only anxiety issues that Cognitive Restructuring can play a positive role. Boelen et al (2007), showed that Cognitive Restructuring combined with Exposure Therapy, successfully helped in bereavement interventions (4.2b). This approach helped to reduce the effects of grief

The capacity to store memories is an amazing function. It helps to guide us safely through our lives. We refer to past-experiences when making choices and decisions. Through those memories, we make assumptions about what will happen in any given situation. If we have had a bad experience, that memory will fixate itself into our minds. Difficulties can then arise when faced with the same or similar situation. As our anxiety increases because of a bad memory, we tend to blow the memory out of all proportion. This can escalate into a downward spiral of anxiety. Let's suppose that the past-experience is analyzed through Cognitive Restructuring. When confronting a similar situation in the future, you will approach it more positively.

The intent is to identify the negative thoughts and challenge them. By modifying the irrationality that you have given them, you will start to realize the truth of your negative assessment. Remember that how you think affects how you feel. By turning that thought into a good one, it will improve your overall wellbeing.

For example. You are standing in a remote train station waiting for a train. You are feeling alone and vulnerable. Your heart is racing and you begin to feel afraid, even though there are no actual signs of danger. This, in turn, sets off negative thoughts, such as,

"What if someone attacks me?" Once this thought takes a grip, it can be difficult to shake the feeling of peril. Now you are feeling anxious.

If you can learn to recognize when this happens, you will have the control to realize that your thoughts are irrational. Only then can you try to turn those negative cognitions into positive ones. Force yourself to think positively regarding your situation. Look at the good in the situation, such as, "This place is surrounded by nature and it's beautiful." "Sitting here waiting is so peaceful and relaxing."

Already your mind is healing as you replace the maladaptive thoughts with positive ones. To help in this process you could try using a relaxing technique, such as the breathing exercise. If you are successful, it will help if you are ever in a similar situation again. Instead of it inducing anxiety, you will seek the positives in your situation and take strength from them. If you're memories of remain negative, you may inadvertently take the route of avoidance and never visit that station again. As we have already discussed, avoidance only helps to reinforce Cognitive Distortions. Even if nothing bad ever happened in that place, you convince yourself that you are going to be the first victim. You magnify the whole experience and turn it into a negative situation.

There are many techniques used by Cognitive Restructuring. All ways of helping you challenge a bad situation.

Decatastrophizing

Also known as the 'What if' technique. This method uses mental imagery. It is used on patients suffering from Cognitive Distortions. They will be encouraged to think about the most severe outcome of the situation or object that has caused their anxiety. This helps to determine if the patient has over exaggerated the threat. At the same time, it will show them if they have underestimated their ability to cope.

Thought Awareness

This method targets being aware of the Cognitive Distortions that cause the anxiety. By pulling out the memories mentally, it helps to understand how and why they cause maladaptive thinking. It can be difficult, especially if when in the middle of a panic attack. Trying to unpick the thought processes that brought on the anxiety is a mentally painful process. It is useful for determining triggers that bring on the feelings of unease and panic.

Socratic Questioning

This is using a set routine for questioning maladaptive thoughts. It's named after the Greek Philosopher, Socrates. He argued that through systematic questioning we can understand and deconstruct ideas. In turn, this will either verify those ideas or dismiss them. With Socratic questioning, it is necessary to first identify the Cognitive Distortions. With logical questioning, it will either lend clarification to the patient's theory or challenge it.

Thoughts appear as dialogue in our minds, along with a few visual images. A trained therapist will encourage patients to share negative thoughts. Then, they will ask questions that might challenge such thoughts.

Typical self-questions could be:

- Are the thoughts you are having based on feelings or facts? What evidence do you have that verify your opinion?

- Is there an alternative explanation of how you are seeing a situation? If there is, how would that change the way you now feel?

- What are the consequences of the situations you perceive, and what is the best or worst case outcome? How will you cope with those outcomes?

- Will other people have the same answers to that thought as you do? If not, why would they come to different conclusions?

- Are you looking at only the black and white areas, and not seeking the grey parts?

-

There are no correct answers to such questions. It is a means of unraveling maladaptive thinking. This sort of session should help the patient to analyze their negative thoughts. Helping to bring out the reasons why they think them. Then helping to defuse such thoughts.

This method also shows the patient how to question their own irrational fears. Socrates questioning does not necessarily need two people. Once the patient has been shown how to question themselves, they can use it on their own negative thoughts.

3. Behavioral Experiments

We have discussed the benefits of altering thoughts in helping to control anxiety. Now we will move on to behavioral experiments, which involves acting out thoughts. This process helps to reinforce the positives from the thought exercise. It is about re-enacting the negative thoughts in a real situation to study the outcome.

When an anxious person asks themselves "what if," it can start a spiral of anxiety. behavioral experiments on thought exercises can help them see that the outcome may not be as bad as they expected. By using behavioral experiments, the patient can act out that "what if" scenario to see that the result may, in fact, be a positive one.

It is a way of testing out the hypothesis raised by the patient on the imaginary "what if" situation. This is a common therapy for CBT and there are variations to carry out the experiments. It is about testing for and against a worrisome anxious situation, by role-playing the different scenarios.

To begin with, it should start with the help of the therapist, or even in group therapy session. It can also involve going out into a public setting to enact the theory. At the same time, the patient will have a worksheet to record their emotions, feelings, and thoughts both before and after the experiment. This is to reflect upon later, so the patient can see the exact outcome of their imagined anxiety.

It is not only about analyzing the outcomes, but it is also about learning coping strategies. Through the role-play method, the patient is encouraged to cope with situations they find difficult.

Let's use an example to play this out:

> Jenny hates going to the store. It is gradually got worse when the store was busy. To start with, she would try to go on quiet days. But she began to imagine everyone was watching her, or the store staff looked at her as though she was going to steal something. It became so difficult for Jenny that she slowly stopped going to any stores.

The behavior exercise could begin in a group session, with people she knows acting as the customers. She could think up situations that worry her, such as a customer staring at her. Between herself, her therapist and the others in the group, they could decide how she could approach the person looking at her, in a calm way. Perhaps she could smile at them and say "hi," but the thought of doing this scares her. If she can manage to do it in the group, eventually she may be able to do it in the store. Later in the program, her therapist will take her to a small store. The group members may join them and enact the scenario out in public. This way, Jenny gets to do her role-playing in a public setting.

What can Jenny learn through her behavioral experiment?

- Jenny will be encouraged to write notes about her feelings and anxiety levels.
- This is a controlled way to confront those dreaded "what ifs?"
- Building up confidence through role play.
- Practicing assertion.
- Learning how to approach and talk to a stranger in a calm manner.
- More importantly, Jenny is learning coping mechanisms for situations that she fears. If it does happen and some stranger stares at her when she is alone, she will now know how to deal with it without embarrassing herself.

By exposing Jenny to her dreaded thoughts, it has shown her that even if the worse was to happen, she can still cope with it. It is a form of exposure treatment, but it is also so much more. Jenny could practice eye contact during group sessions to help build up confidence in approaching other people. In their role play as customers, the others in the group can put her on the spot. They could ask her which row the bread is on. She would need to create an image in her head of a shop and put herself visually in the rows to create an answer. All helping to put her in a situation she has not been able to cope with.

It is a way of building up a picture of something the patient dreads, and then confronts it. All the while, the patient is supported and encouraged.

Of course, it cannot cover life-threatening situations. It is more for dealing with social anxiety, such as asking for directions, eating in public, or going in an escalator. All such fears that can be overcome with behavioral exercises.

Successive Approximation

It also lends the patient another coping mechanism of Successive Approximation. They are learning to break a huge problem into smaller pieces. Each step of the way will get harder and they cannot move forward until they have successfully achieved the previous step. The reward is a mental one; they can move on to the next stage until they achieve their final goal. What better reward is there than that. It shows the patient that if they continue to practice breaking down problems in a similar fashion, such as note taking and analysing those notes to move on, they can find a way to tackle their anxieties as they happen.

Worksheet Ideas

This is a way of encouraging and recording a patient's feelings of dread. It is in the form of an experiment that is first rehearsed in role play.

Sometimes it may end there, or it may go on to be carried out in public, but in a controlled setting.

Taking the example we used in the chapter, here's what type of questions could go onto this experiment log sheet.

Q. What is the Fear?

A. Unable to go into stores for fear of being judged.

Q. What do you think will happen in the stores?

A. People stare at me and shop assistants look at me suspiciously like I'm a shoplifter.

Q. How do you see Design of the Experiment playing out.

A.

- Roleplay in group sessions to include other customer reactions in a store.

- Followed by role-play in a public setting, to include other members of the group and the therapist.

The log sheet should be designed around the individual experiment. The client can then record each session, logging their feelings as the dreaded situation plays out. In the case study, we have suggested it could be as follows:

Session 1:

Q. What is the role play?

A, Group members play customers. One will ask me where an item is in the imaginary shop. We have agreed beforehand to base it on a local store that we know. I am to describe where the item is. I will visually imagine myself standing by the main entrance. Then I will explain to the customer how to get to the right row.

Q. What are your feelings Before, During and After the experiment?

A.

- Before: I felt embarrassed at the role play.
- During: I had heart palpitations and difficulty breathing because I was thinking about being in the store.
- After: I felt more confident because the "customer" smiled at me and thanked me. It went well thanks to my group.

Session 2:

Q. What was the role play?

A group member played a shopper who stared at me as I walked around tables that represented store shelves. I had set questions that were considered as the "norm, that myself and the group agreed upon. I approached the group member "shopper," with these questions to help me deal with talking to her.

Q. What were your feelings Before, During and After the experiment?

A.

- Before: I was uncomfortable as the group member watched me walking around the tables. I had been encouraged to visualize myself in the store and that's what unbalanced me.
- During: In the past, I would have left the store. This time I asked the set questions that I would not have thought up by myself. They were comfortable questions, such as, "you look familiar, do we know each other?" It forced the other person to speak to me, which I was dreading. The aim was to ask a question that is friendly and maybe force a friendly reaction. I was okay in the role play but not sure I can follow this through in a real life.
- After: I like the idea of thinking up friendly questions. If someone stares at me, I might dare myself to ask them where to find

something. That way I can see if they act strangely towards me.

Session 3:

Q. What was the role play?

A. Those involved in my group went with me to a small store. We enacted the role-play that we'd done in the sessions.

Q. What were your feelings Before the experiment, During and After?

We can't give real answers and results to this experiment, as it is imaginary. The purpose is to give you an idea of how to go about a behavioral experiment. It is all about role-playing out those dreaded "what ifs," rather than just thinking about them. The group therapy should always be supervised by a professional therapist to achieve the best results. It is meant to guide the client towards possible ways to overcome the reasons for their anxiety.

4. Pleasant Activity Scheduling (AS)

This technique is a type of Behavioral treatment but does not involve role-playing. It is more about the patient influencing their own Behavioral Activation System (BAS)

.

The BAS is part of a hypothesis advocated in 1970, by British Psychologist Jeffrey Gray. Based on physiological responses, it is known as the Biopsychological Theory of Personality. Today, it is a widely-accepted conjecture within the psychological disciplines.

There are two main facets to this motivational neural model. One is the Behavioral Inhibition System (BIS), and the other is BAS. Each system is activated by different situations.

- The BIS leads to the negative stimuli of punishment and avoidance.
- The BAS leads to more positive stimuli, such as motivation and rewards.

Gray argued that BIS is the initial cause of anxiety.

Pleasant Activity Scheduling (AS) is primarily used for depression. It can also have benefits for those who suffer from the symptoms of anxiety. A study by Chu, et al (2009), indicates that students suffering from anxiety and or depression, received clinical benefits from BAS (4.4a). Using "AS" as a treatment for anxiety involves planning engaging activities. By doing so, it will result in the patient having positive experiences to look forward to. In a sense, patients are rewarding themselves. This is particularly useful for PTSD sufferers.

AS discourages isolation. It is aimed at getting patients to engage in positive activities to keep their minds active in a constructive way. Tailoring the events around the anxiety issues is an effective part of the course. For instance, if you are nervous about the sea, don't go on a boat trip. Unlike Exposure Therapy where you would need to face your fears, this is more about seeking pleasure to result in positive thinking. Even the planning can be an exciting part of the experience. Sometimes the build-up to an event can invoke happiness. The patient will be thinking about what they are looking forward to. This creates a better means of inner reflection to the normal negative anxious irrationalities.

By increasing activity levels, there is less opportunity to brood over negative thoughts. The planning and the taking part in PA, are all distracting the thought process away from maladaptive thinking. Instead, it forces the patient to focus on positive and happier contemplations. AS should be taken at a pace the patient is comfortable with, and not rushed. Whether it includes only one activity planned in a week, or several activities, is not the key issue. In fact, it is better not to over plan, risking the possibility of panic. The point is to pull away from the normal environment and experience a feel-good factor

For instance, if you are stuck in your home most of the time, then imagine the great sense of achievement at getting to go out and about. Particularly so if you end up enjoying it.

For a patient suffering from depression, this therapy would be aimed at making them feel more motivated. It should serve to increase their energy drive and push them forward. For anxiety though, it is more used as a distraction. It works by pulling the patient away from their daily negative thinking patterns, that they are so often trapped within.

It is not for everyone. For some, it may not be an

easy type of exercise, though it is not done alone. A therapist will instruct a patient on how best to go about AS, though there will be many exercises encouraged as homework.

When choosing activities, it is good to choose healthy ones, here are a few suggestions. They won't suit everyone so feel free to add your own:

- Going out in the evening with a friend, maybe to the movies.
- Booking a sauna or message, a great way to help relax your body.
- Swimming, or joining an exercise class such as yoga.
- Going out for a "nature day" such as bird watching or strolling around a forest or lake.
- Booking a sports session such as badminton or tennis with a friend at a gym, or playing basketball.
- Going to a beach for the day.
- Joining a local group, ie book or gardening

club.

If you don't feel ready to go out and plan such energetic activities, then alternatively, plan to get stuff done around the home. Make sure you are achieving so many tasks in a week to give yourself a sense of satisfaction, such as:

- Starting a hobby, ie card making, knitting, jigsaw puzzles.
- Gardening can be therapeutic and a great way to get yourself outside and fit.
- Bake, cakes, cupcakes biscuit and pies, whatever takes your fancy. Beware of the calories. Though you could always donate your baking to a charitable cause, a great way to lift your self-esteem.
- Having a luxurious soak in the bathtub with candles.
- If money is an issue for you, then take a serious look at your finances. By planning

ahead, you may find yourself better off financially.

- Get up an hour earlier to get more done.

Whatever way you choose to approach your Activity Scheduling (AS), it is important that it gives you pleasure or satisfaction. AS is meant to serve as your own self-reward. If you plan to tackle that bill-paying session, the feel-good factor should come from knowing that you are tackling a problem. That, in itself, can ease anxiety. Plus, if you are addressing such problems, keep the time devoted to these tasks short. Problems are solved much better if broken up into smaller pieces.

Don't just include outside activities, add things that you keep putting off so you can have a sense of self-achievement. This type of therapy ties up well with creating a routine in your life. By planning some good things ahead, that you can do with your time, you will have less time to dwell on those negative anxious thoughts.

5. Mindfulness-based Cognitive Therapy (MBCT)

"A man is but the product of his thoughts. What he thinks, he becomes."—
Mahatma Gandhi

Mindfulness is an activity often more related to Buddhist monks. Some may also relate it to the ancient practice of yoga. It is also a useful tool in CBT for treating stress-related disorders and anxiety. Whilst it is a meditative practice, it can help anyone to learn to focus on the inner self.

We are all capable of visually seeing what happens around us, but many of us cannot see what is happening within. By becoming more aware of your inner thoughts you can analyze how they fit into the world around you. It teaches you how to study your own emotions and question the reasons why you react to certain things. If you are more aware, then you can make better judgments. It is generally being aware of the 'self' in the "here and now that Mindfulness will help you to focus on.

Mindfulness has shown to be effective in helping to treat anxiety, stress, and depression. Goldin & Gross (2010) carried out a study on participants who suffered from Social Anxiety Disorder (SAD) (4.5a). The results indicated that their symptoms were reduced whilst participating in mindfulness exercises.

American professor, emeritus of medicine, Jon-Kabat Zin is the pioneer of Mindfulness-Based Stress Reduction (MBSR) (4.5b). He opened a Stress Reduction clinic in 1979. It runs 8-week courses on Mindfulness-based Cognitive Therapy, based on MBSR. MBSR uses a combination of mindfulness meditation, yoga, and personal body awareness. This helps to treat issues such as pain management, anxiety and also reduces stress. MBSR has proven to be so effective that mindfulness meditation is taught in almost 80% of all medical schools in the US.

People mostly react automatically to stimulus, often not giving much thought to their response. This is known as Automatic Negative Thoughts (ANTs).

For Example Road rage can develop from a very minor incident. Perhaps someone cuts you up on the highway and you automatically sound your horn. Why have you done this? It is not meant to be used aggressively. Yet, you are letting the driver know you are not happy with what they have done. This can further develop into a more aggressive situation. You then speed-up to catch them.

Further, you then outstare them or even worse, you might force them to stop and physically confront them. The behavior serves no purpose. Instead, you will succeed in raising your own blood pressure and elevating your stress levels as your anger increases.

The exaggerated behavior developed from your unconsciousness. That is because it is a part of your automatic thought process. A reaction you have developed over the years for a disagreeable event. The incidence led to your thoughts becoming fuelled by your emotions. In turn, this led to your aggressive behavior.

MBCT sessions would help you to become more aware of your present senses, and avoid such scenes in the future. You will learn to recognize certain indicators. The fact that your heart speeds up and you grip at the wheel tightly, should alert you to the imminent danger. Because you have learned to look out for such signals, you will no longer respond automatically. Instead, you will purposely intervene and alter your reaction. it will give you the power to hold back on your previous aggressive behavior. Your alternative thinking will be more on the terms of: The guy cut out in front of me but he's done it now. No point exploding with anger and making myself ill when it won't change that fact. Your new automatic reaction will be to take some deep breaths and force your hands to relax on the wheel.

Relaxation Exercises in MBCT

By using basic meditation exercises, it empowers you to ease any imminent anxiety attacks.

Breathing 4-7-8

This is a relaxation method that you can use anywhere, anytime. Though it is also a form of yogic breathing as it leads to relaxation for a meditation session. It's always better if you can lay down, or sit, but you can do it standing up if that becomes necessary.

- Close your eyes if possible. It helps to shut out the visual noise that you can see.
- Inhale deeply through your nostrils for the count of 4.
- As you inhale, allow your abdomen to expand, you will find that your chest also rises.
- Hold the breath for the count of 7.
- Gently exhale the air through an open mouth for the count of 8.
- Repeat this process until you feel a calmness.
- Use different rates of counting if 4-7-8 doesn't work for you or makes you feel dizzy.

It can take a while to adjust the "count" to your own body but 4-7-8 is a general rule of thumb. The hardest part is focussing on cutting out the busy world around you. Once you achieve this skill you will be capable of switch off momentarily. Not only will the panic pass over but you should also experience an inner peace.

A study by Brown & Gerbarg (2005), show that at least 30 minutes of daily yogic exercise a day, helps to reduce the symptoms of stress, anxiety and PTSD (4.5c).

Progressive Muscle Relaxation

This is another exercise that will have better results if you can lay down. Though it can be done seated or standing up if you find yourself in a stressful situation, but there will be limitations.

The idea behind this technique is to relax muscles in your body. It is also known as a body scan as you can start from the bottom of the body to the top, or vice versa. It is always better if you begin any exercise by using the breathing method to begin with.

- Close your eyes if possible to shut out the visual noise that you can see.
- Inhale deeply through your nose, hold for a few seconds before exhaling through your mouth.
- Concentrate on your feet. Flex and wiggle them, tighten any muscles. Move the toes and turn the ankles.
- If you have the time, complete the breathing exercise before moving on to the next muscle group, though it isn't necessary if you don't.
- Next, think only about your lower legs and calves, tensing and then relaxing any muscles in that area.
- Use this method to work your way through your body until you arrive at your face.
- Tighten any muscles in the face area by screwing up your eyes and wiggling your nose. Open the jaws wide a few times and gently wiggle it from side to side. Feel your face muscles relaxing as you do so.

- Finish with a few deep breathing exercises before you open your eyes to the world around you.

If you do this in public you may find yourself only focusing on a few muscle groups. At least you are shifting your thoughts from the anxiety and focusing on the inner self. That is the whole intention, to try and eliminate those negative thoughts by using a deep meditative means of relaxation.

Such exercises will have a positive effect on your wellbeing.

6. Altering Negative Thought Patterns

Low Self Esteem

It is not unusual to find that a person suffering from anxiety, will also usually suffer from low self-esteem. The chances are they have put themselves down in their own minds. This is a natural way of thinking as their confidence has diminishes. Low self-self-esteem can be a direct result of maladaptive thoughts.

There are some steps that you can take to try and overcome negative thought patterns. Let's have a look at a few of these ideas:

A trigger point can occur simply by you perceiving a remark by someone else, to be negative. If you find yourself feeling upset at another's remark, learn to recognize why you are upset. Take action by not allowing the maladaptive thought to fester. Don't give it time to build up, as this can create a snowball effect of anxiety. One way to do that is to try and relax internally. Use the breathing techniques we discussed earlier. Even if it's only to close your eyes for a few seconds. Try and at least inhale one deep breath through your nose, and exhale the air through your mouth. It is enough to take your mind away from an instant automatic reaction.

Case Scenario:

Let's suppose you are in a meeting and feel excited at doing your own presentation. Your mood is good and positive. Then someone comes at you with what you perceive as an insulting remark. Whilst you take that deep breath, think about the situation you are in. To help you understand why the remark triggered a negative thought ask yourself: -

- Is it the person rather than the remark?
- Would you have felt the same no matter who had said that same remark?
- Have they actually made a valid point?
- Did you experience a mood swing as soon as the trigger point happened?

By using our example, we know that the person felt happy and confident only moments before the comment. When they received the negative remark, they felt annoyed and upset.

Automatic Thoughts

If an instant mood swing does happen, it means that you have experienced an "automatic thought. Most automatic thoughts are instant negative responses. Again, be aware and ask yourself: -

- Am I now thinking negative remarks detrimental to my self-confidence, such as "I'm useless at this," or "that person never liked me?"
- Look for evidence in your mind that might support why you had such an automatic negative response.

By asking yourself such questions, it forces you to look objectively at the automatic thought process. Is there any evidence to support why you are now thinking about this person in a negative way? Or, is their point a good one?

The remark caught you unawares and unprepared. Before you use an automatic response, assess the situation in your mind as fast as you can. By learning to see your own trigger points, such as this one, you will know when not to respond immediately. The last thing you want is to come across as aggressive, so stop and think. As you are busy analyzing the situation in your mind, it allows for a short pause. that's a good thing as you are not responding instantly. It brings to mind the saying, "Think before you speak."

Positive Thinking

Bring in some positive thinking too, for example:

- Only one person raised any comments, so that's not too bad.
- I can't be useless if I'm standing here doing a presentation of my ideas.

If you manage to stay calm and answer the question sensibly, then pat yourself on the back. You've managed to challenge those automatic and maladaptive thoughts. Now you can approach the objector calmly and not make a fool of yourself. Your response can be a measured one because you have taken full control of your thinking.

This is only a simple example. It reflects a situation that would need to be performed on the spot, to stop any automatic negativeness.

Beware when you are feeling vulnerable and want to snap at someone for something they said. Pause and ask yourself: -

- Am I having an instant thought and reaction?
- Has what they said caused a swing in my mood and emotions?
- Can I stay calm and smile and stop assuming negative stuff in my head?

If you have decided to do a journal and something like this happens in your day, take notes. What was the situation that forced your automatic negative reaction? What was your instant mood when it happened? How did you deal with it? When you get a chance, look at your notes to analyze them to see if you could have changed anything. Learn from the experience, don't ignore it. Learn to master the process of pausing to analyze. It is a start to your challenging all maladaptive thoughts, in all situations.

7. Anxiety in Childhood

We have discussed how adults can challenge negative thought patterns that lead to anxious thoughts. What then of children? Can a child suffer from anxiety?

The answer to that is, yes. Whilst it's quite difficult to gain exact scientific data from this age group, nonetheless, children do suffer from anxiety. One such study by Muris and Broeren (2009) (4.7a), looked at research taken over 25 years. The results indicated that in fact anxiety disorders, including

PTSD, OCD, and social phobias, are on the increase for the young. Given this daunting news, how can we help our children to cope with a condition that few adults can manage to handle?

How do you know if your own child is suffering from anxious moments?

There are a few signs in a child's behavior that could indicate anxiety is present.

- Tiredness that is probably due to lack of sleep.
- Suffering panicky scared feelings for much of the time.
- Lack of concentration, leading to poor school performance.
- Misbehaving.
- Taking tantrums.
- Bullying other children.
- Withdrawal from play.

- Constant complaints of tummy aches or headaches.

Some of these symptoms can also be signs of general childhood ailments. Though if they are frequent and persistent, then anxiety may be the cause.

Anxiety is the most common mental health ailment for young people. Community studies show that between 9-32% of children and adolescents suffer some form of anxiety disorder. (Creswell, Waite & Cooper 2014) (4.7b). This can and does have an adverse effect on their development. The research sadly indicates that anxiety in childhood can continue into adulthood. Anxiety issues affect a child's family life, social development, and educational achievement. It can even result in dependence on welfare and low paid employment, later in adulthood. (Piacentini & Robleck 2002) (4.7c). Many children suffering from anxiety disorders go untreated because the symptoms are so variable.

Genes also play their part in anxiety. Studies are showing that if you have a close relative suffering a Generalized Anxiety Disorder (GAD), then you are seven times more likely to suffer it too. (Turner, Beildal & Costello 1987) (4.7d). Genetics do not offer a complete explanation. The social environment of a child plays a huge role. For example, if children witness their parents' anxious behavior, they are more likely to mirror such emotions. Difficult and upsetting experiences are another factor. That can include the death of a family member or a loved pet, or being subject to violence or abuse. These situations can lead to PTSD, which can have a devastating effect on anyone, let alone a child. There is a range of specific, seemingly innocuous moments in a child's life, that can result in the onset of anxiety. Such as Separation Anxiety when starting school. Most children do well in a good routine, so when their regular day altered, it can cause them anxieties.

How do we treat anxiety in children?

Treatment for children is not that different to the treatment for adults. The premise is the same; identify maladaptive thoughts and challenge them. Intervention as early as possible is more likely to see a better success rate from the treatment. Delayed treatment carries a risk of the child becoming isolated. If that happens they may become unable to cope and fall behind in their development.

Supportive parents, teachers, and friends play a major role in a child's life. Learning to recognize a child's trigger points is a great way forward in therapy. To do this, some children may be treated with Exposure therapy. It does not need to be a direct exposure, as in-vivo exposure. A more suitable method for children is imaginal exposure. It is useful in helping to alter maladaptive thinking, the same way as it does for adults.

Providing support to talk about and confront their fears is another method. It encourages them to discuss their fears with you, so together you can find solutions to reduce that fear.

Other treatment options include Modeling. This is where a model, usually the therapist, acts out the behavior which is causing the anxiety in the child. The child learns by observations, though Modeling alone has a short-term effectiveness. When combined with role-play and positive reinforcement exercises, it is more successful. Role-play is a way of rehearsing with coping mechanisms. It will involve challenging the negative thoughts and at the same time rewarding the child for correct behavior. this has been taken forward with the use of computer-assisted CBT. A study by Khanna & Kendall (2010) (4.7e), showed that by using computer-aided CBT with children, it was very effective in reducing anxiety.

CBT has proven to be a useful treatment for children, even very young children. A study by Minde et. al. (2010) (4.7d), shows that children between the ages of 3-7 suffering anxiety disorders can still benefit with CBT.

In a clinical setting, they will build their skills in altering thought patterns. The patients will also be given tasks for homework, where their supporters can become involved too. Parents can also be directed into changing their approach to the child. They too may need to learn new tactics and coping strategies. Considering that parents are the role models, it is important to train them as well.

With the use of CBT, the patient can look forward to a quick recovery. By the end of a few months of therapy sessions, the child should learn new coping strategies for their future. The average therapy sessions required can be between 8-16. Some patients may need more, dependent on the severity of their symptoms. With the coping skills taught in CBT, and support from immediate family members, the outlook for these children is very good. That is not true though for a child who goes untreated. The likelihood is that they will continue to suffer anxiety and maladaptive thoughts. Untreated, their condition will most likely get worse as they get older.

Chapter 5 Exposure Therapy

Anxious Fears

Exposure therapy is a CBT technique used for helping people who suffer various anxiety disorders and phobias. Research of this technique has shown that when provided by a skilled practitioner it is both effective and safe.

Exposure therapy is used mainly to treat:

- Post-Traumatic Stress Disorder (PTSD)
- Panic attacks
- Obsessive-compulsive Disorder (OCD)
- Social Anxiety Disorder (SAD)
- Generalized Anxiety Disorder (GAD)

The history of exposure therapy predates CBT. It was initially a method of treatment prescribed by behavioral psychologists. The foundation of which was based on classical conditioning. The most famous classical conditioning experiment was Ivan

Pavlov's experiment with dogs. He conditioned them to salivate at the sound of a bell, as that preceded the introduction of food.

Behavioral psychologists, such as B.F. Skinner, took this principle further. The introduction of operant conditioning was an additional concept of modifying certain behaviors. Skinner believed behavior was determined by consequences, whether good or bad. The consequences then determine if the behavior continues, or not. Positive consequences result in reinforcing the behavior. Whilst negative consequences would, for most people, result in the cessation of such behavior.

It was Mary Cover Jones, often described as the mother of behavior therapy, who introduced the concept of desensitization. This is a process of repeatedly exposing a person to the stimulus that is the cause their anxiety. Today we know this as exposure therapy.

Fear is a powerful emotion. When we fear something, it is only natural that we try and avoid it. For certain situations it is acceptable, such as you would not confront a big bear on purpose. In a more realistic setting, some people may be frightened of driving at excessive speeds so avoid that situation. Another reasonable and practical fear. It is when your fears focus on the more mundane situations that it is considered a problematic type of fear. Perhaps being in an enclosed space, or being in a crowd. Avoiding everyday situations can have a detrimental effect on your quality of life. Avoiding situations that make you unwell, may at first seem the right thing to do. It seems a sensible option to help ease your anxious feelings. What such avoidance is really doing though, is reinforcing the fear. If you don't tackle the problematic fear, you can never overcome it.

Exposure therapy is intent on breaking that cycle of avoidance so that it will not be so maladaptive. This type of therapy has variations of methods. They are tailored by the therapist to suit the individual's needs.

Common Exposure Methods

In-Vivo Exposure

A treatment path which directly exposes the suffer to the stimuli. This would be carried out under the supervision of a trained therapist and is about confronting the fear. An example could be a client who has an inhibiting fear of flying. One aspect of the treatment could involve them visiting an airport and actually boarding a plane. They will not do this alone as they will be accompanied by a trained therapist. Throughout the event the client is encouraged to practice calming techniques, such as controlled breathing.

Interoceptive Exposure

A technique whereby the therapist induces physical sensations. This is encouraging the client to think about and describe their fear. Such physical feelings may include shortness of breath, muscle tension, and a racing heartbeat. The purpose is to show that these sensations, while uncomfortable, are not actually dangerous.

Imaginal Exposure

Often used in a complementary fashion to In Vivo Exposure. The difference being that it uses Imaginal Exposure. The client is not exposed directly to the situation that causes their anxiety. Instead, they are encouraged to visualize the traumatic fear. Similar to Interoceptive Exposure, the intent is to provoke the feelings of anxiety.

Virtual Reality Exposure

This is a new technique. It involves immersing the patient in a virtual reality environment, usually with a headset. It is ideal for exposing a client to certain situations that they perceive as dangerous in the real world. Particularly useful for those suffering PTSD and has been successful with combat veterans.

An important element to using exposure therapy is determining the level of exposure to the anxiety-inducing stimuli. Too much too soon may be damaging to the client. There are three basic methods of determining exposure levels in CBT.

Systematic Desensitization

Exposure to the anxiety-inducing stimuli, while engaging in stress-reducing activities. This would include exercises such as controlled breathing, or other relaxation techniques.

Graded Exposure

With the help of the therapist, the client is asked to construct a hierarchal list of anxiety-inducing situations. This treatment will involve exposing the client to the less threatening fears first. Then, a build-up to the more difficult situations at a gradual pace.

Flooding

This is a more aggressive and somewhat controversial method of exposure therapy. That is because this method overwhelms the client with anxiety-inducing stimuli. Whilst it can only be used on a limited number of clients, it is perhaps the most cost-effective and quickest method. It has proven to help cure phobias and other anxiety issues.

Does exposure therapy work?

There has been a plethora of studies showing this method of therapy is successful in helping people with anxiety issues. How successful it is for each individual person, is dependent on the therapist's approach. One such study by Rothbaum & Schwartz (2002) (5a), demonstrates that it is successful in treating PTSD. For most, a gradual approach is key to success. If it is not rushed into it and taken one step at a time, the patient can overcome the sense of dread that they feel.

Following are some examples of how different techniques in exposure therapy can help treat PTSD:

PTSD Sufferers have either been the victim of a traumatic event or witnessed one. Typical symptoms of PTSD can include repetitive disturbing thoughts and frightening nightmares. As they play the event over in their minds, it can make them hyper-vigilant, (always on the lookout for danger). All these symptoms can lead to depression.

Like most anxiety issues, those suffering from PTSD can take the same route for relief, which is often avoidance. This is counter-productive, as avoidance reinforces the fear, it can also lead to other problems. Those supplementary issues can include emotional detachment from others, even loved ones. Along with a lack of interest in life and again depression will set in. Exposure therapy for PTSD can take many forms. By using that various techniques we have mentioned earlier, see how they fit in to a PTSD patient's therapy:

In-Vivo Exposure

The patient is exposed to the event that causes the anxiety. This might involve visiting the scene of the traumatic event. For example, someone involved in a violent incident could visit the place where it happened. A professional therapist will guide them to challenge the feelings that arise. It must be a supervised situation as the patient can become overwhelmed, needing to leave the scene immediately.

Imaginal Exposure

If the patient is not yet ready to face the scene of the event, then this is a safer option. Instead, the patient uses imaginary techniques to relive the traumatic experience. It will be necessary to relive the experiences in their mind. Along with a professional therapist who will help them to challenge the thoughts and feelings that this memory can bring about.

Interoceptive Exposure

A typical symptom of PTSD can come in the form of a panic attacks. Such attacks are often in response to a physical sensation, such as a racing heart, or shortness of breath. With this technique, the therapist will try and induce those feelings. This is done by encouraging the patient to hyperventilate. It can be used in conjunction with Imaginal Exposure. The patient not only imagines the event but is also experiencing induced hyperventilation. A study by Wald & Taylor (2008) (5b), shows that Interoceptive Exposure is effective in reducing anxiety in PTSD sufferers.

Virtual Reality Exposure

This method is becoming increasingly popular. Most especially for treating armed forces veterans, as well as active soldiers. PTSD is a known condition that can be brought on by combat memories. It is about replicating anxiety-inducing scenarios, without placing the client in physical danger. This can involve immersing the client into a virtual reality world that is created with powerful computers. The patient experiences not only a visual world but also other senses too. It will include audio, and sometimes sensory awareness of touch. The visual and audio sensations are translated via a headset. Whilst the sensory sensations are experienced by sensors placed around the patient's body. Like all exposure therapy, the intention is to repeatedly expose the client to the anxiety-inducing stimuli. Eventually, the autonomic arousal that is a causal factor in panic attacks, is subdued. This is known as "habituation." Virtual Reality Exposure has shown to be successful in helping PTSD suffers. It works at reducing the severity of their PTSD symptoms.

Exposure therapy is a useful tool at helping to treat those who suffer PTSD. It can also help with other anxiety issues, such as phobias and Obsessive Compulsive Disorders. The various techniques offer ways to challenge the maladaptive thought process. In the long run, it helps patients to come to terms with the trauma that caused the illness in the first place. The origins of this type of therapy are based on older forms of behavioral psychology. But, as in Virtual Reality Exposure, it has been developed to help patients deal with modern day issues. All of which are possible with by the new state of the art technology.

Chapter 6 Formulating and executing a personalized plan

Self Help Treatment for Anxiety Disorders

If you are an anxious person and it affects your life in a debilitating way, then you do need to take action. The best way forward would be to seek a professional CBT therapist. If for some reason you cannot take that route, such as financial reasons or time, then there are alternatives. One option is self-help. This can be successful for none-extreme anxiety issues. Self-help healing has shown to be effective and can help to change your life around. (Hirai & Clum 2006, (6a). It is worth pursuing if only for your loved ones. Though, at the end of the day, you are the important one in this dilemma.

Remind yourself that you are not alone with your condition. The Anxiety and Depression Association of America (ADAA), informs us that around 15 million Americans suffer from Generalized Anxiety

Disorder (GAD). On top of that, around 7.7 million Americans suffer PTSD. In the US 40% of adults will suffer from an anxiety disorder at some time in their lives (ADAA 2013) (6b).

By becoming your own therapist you are taking the first step to tackling your anxiety issues. Depression can be a more difficult condition to tackle because of its deep routed causes, but self-help can still be useful. A meta-analysis of 34 studies by Gellatly et. al. (2006) (6c), looked at the effectiveness of self-help for depression. They found that self-help could successfully reduce the symptoms.

CBT involves learning ways of challenging the negative thoughts the lead to anxiety. Further practice is then required for a well-balanced mental health outlook. By reading books like this one you may have already identified that you are experiencing a problem you want to deal with. After all, this is not a topic that makes good bedtime reading. However, by reading material on CBT therapy, you have made the right start.

CBT is such a logical way of tackling anxiety issues. That is because it forces the practitioner to face their anxieties and do something about them. Once you have admitted that you need to tackle some issues you are having, then it is time to move on:

- What are your negative inner thoughts?
- Whilst focusing on those thoughts, note the moods and emotions you feel whilst you are thinking them.
- Compare your moods to how you feel when you're not thinking those thoughts.
- Learn how to dissect such thoughts, as discussed in the various CBT methods throughout this book.

Research and Reading Material

There is a rich variety of reading materials around, both online and in physical book format. Read about the different CBT methods, such as the breathing techniques. Then have a go at putting them into practice.

Putting a CBT Method into Practice

Find a CBT technique that suits you, such as writing a journal which is ideal for busy people. Writing a contemporaneous daily record allows you to read it later on. This allows you to reflect on situations that made you anxious during your day. Did something happen at the office that upset you? If you had a chance to log down your thoughts at the time, later when you have calmed down you can analyze why it made you anxious and take action.

Time Management

The word "management" can bring to mind something you do in a working situation, but you can implement this into your personal life. Studies show that having an organized life can bring about a feeling of fulfillment.

Those who suffer anxious moments should avoid being disorganized and rushing about everywhere. Rushing can lead to stress, which in turn starts a whole set of negative thoughts and emotions.

You do not need to have a strict regime, just one whereby your day is a little automated and everything gets done. Here are a few tips that can make a difference and give you empowerment of your life.

Rise earlier than you need to so you can begin your day half asleep. There is nothing worse than diving out of bed and rushing out of the house. Take your time while still dressed in your night clothes. Allow your brain to wake up at a slow pace. Have breakfast early, while you're still waking up. Lead on to a fresh shower and getting ready for the day. Lay your clothes out the day before so you don't need to think in the morning. By the time you leave your home, you will be refreshed and ready to embark on your journey to work.

If you need to travel, plan ahead. Look up the route and give yourself plenty of time. Remember, it is about being as calm and relaxed as possible.

Try to get into the habit of doing a week's meal planning, and then shopping only once during the week. That way everything is worked out ahead and you don't need to rush around when you get home. Plus, you will probably eat healthier if you think about the meals, rather than rushing into a take-out on the way home.

Problem solving

We all need to solve problems at various times in our lives. Sometimes they are the simplest of problems, such as what to wear. Other times they may be more life-changing. None of us can avoid having to make decisions. Most of the time it comes naturally.

When you have other factors in your life, such as money worries, making decisions can become a dreaded and difficult task. Train yourself to tackle problems by breaking them down into smaller portions. For example, if you are worrying that you can't pay all the bills, then you will soon become overwhelmed by the situation. Whereas, if you take the time to prioritize the bills, then action one at a time, you will begin to feel that you are tackling the overall situation.

It's important to keep on top of your life so you feel in control. If, for instance, you are avoiding a particular route to work because it is stressful, then practice Exposure Therapy. Introduce yourself to the route when it's not so busy. Maybe you could take a friend with you for the first time, for moral support.

Learn how to match up the different CBT methods to your own personal anxieties. That way you can begin to take back control of your life. Remember, take your time and don't rush any of the stages.

The Importance of Meditational Exercises

We have talked about this a few times, such as the breathing techniques. If you can incorporate these exercises into your life on a permanent basis, you will soon become familiar with your inner self. That is the person you are ultimately trying to help, so it is worth taking the time to get to know yourself better.

Facing Fears

If you do have phobias then try and get loved ones on board to help you. Don't go around your life avoiding everything. Confront it by using one of the CBT coping strategies. May even take time out of work so you can focus only on tackling the phobia, for a whole week.

CBT Worksheets

There are lots of free worksheets for the varying CBT methods, that can be found online. Do your research and find a few that you feel will be helpful to your particular anxiety. Share them with your loved ones so you have someone to discuss them with.

Key Tasks:

- Recognizing you have a problem.
- Focusing on your inner thoughts and challenging them.
- Finding ways to relax, particularly if you suffer panic attacks.
- Feeling in control of your life.

Then, it is a case of practicing your newfound skills and becoming stronger with your inner self.

Chapter 7 How to move on and continue

Life is one huge challenge, there is no denying that. Formal education in industrialized countries begins at a young age. Along with that comes the pressures to do well in our education. Already we are a part of the social structure of life, there is very little alternative to this way of life. We can have different beliefs and values, but still, the pressure to do well is ever present. Some choose not to live the "norm," but for most of us, we do our best to achieve what is expected of us.

As an adult comes the pressure to do well in a career. Added to that can be the stresses of raising a family, owning a home, a car, and all the latest gadgets that technology provides. We must dress in a certain way, and please our peer groups. This type of social pressure all plays its part upon our personal stress load. Deadlines to meet, places to be, money to earn, bills to pay. It is little wonder that we desire electronic gadgets for entertainment, just to help us unwind.

Whilst social structure is important to us, it does us no harm to step out of the rushing torrent of social expectations, every now and then. We take ourselves on vacation, but even that has to be paid for, organized and traveled to. Being on vacation can be stressful for some. This is where we need to think outside the box.

Most adults arrive at a breaking point sometime in their lives. With the pressures of life comes a price, and that is called stress. It can rear its ugly head in many forms, such as insomnia or eating disorders. The combination of these effects on our bodies floods us with the chemicals meant to protect us from danger. This can be the start of a downward spiral to depression. Of course there are many different reasons for worry and depression, but they all lead to the same result, making us ill.

That's why it's so important to know your own body, including your inner mind; to know yourself. Only then can you recognize the signs that you need help. CBT is a way of providing self-help, which is a great start on the road to recovery. Calming your emotions with meditational exercises is only the first step to healing. Turning around your negative thoughts is a little harder, and takes some time to become successful.

When you've come through a healing session of around 8-weeks, the goal then is to stay healed. There is no point in curing your anxieties only for them to resurface a few months down the line. It is so important to make sure you always recognize when stress is knocking on your door. Nip it in the bud before the symptoms escalate.

Maintaining a Healthy Outlook

If you've read through the chapters of this book, you will have an idea of how anxiety works on the body. How it can snowball into something that can become quite debilitating. When your body perceives a threat, messages go to the brain to produce a response which results in hormonal release. That's fine when faced with danger, it helps to keep you safe as you respond fast. When the body detects danger that is not real, those hormones become toxic.

Take back control by recognizing the signs of a panic attack that is not real. Use the meditational exercises to calm your body's emergency responses. It may sound unreal, but taking charge of your thoughts helps a great deal.

Once you are calmer, the emergency response of hormones will begin to shut down. It may take a few moments as you force your body to change direction, but it can be done. Relax those muscles. Convince your inner thoughts that there is nothing to panic about. Tell yourself that the world is still turning and everything around you remains normal.

Do this over and over until those attacks come less and less. Don't allow maladaptive thoughts to fuel your emotions. When you feel your body going into panic mode, stop whatever you are doing and take action, such as:-

- Close your eyes and start your breathing exercises.
- Visualize pleasant thoughts to distract your mind away from the panic.
- Count numbers in your head and keep counting to distract your mind into the mundane and away from the panic.
- If possible, sit or lay down and then relax go through the motions of tensing and relaxing muscles in your body.

- Go make a cup of tea or coffee to keep your mind distracted.
- Read a book as another form of distracting your thoughts away from the panic.

It is difficult to avoid stress and anxiety completely, but what you can do is recognize it and take action.

Other factors in your life can play a part in making sure that you feel happy inside:

- Spend as much time as you can with loved ones and friends.
- Smile more, even at yourself in the mirror.
- Take more short breaks if your day is a busy one.
- Take a look at your diet and cut down on those sugars and starches as much as you can.
- Take regular exercise, even if it's only walking.
- Visit somewhere pleasant.

- Sit on a bench and watch the world pass you by.
- Go somewhere and interact with nature to recharge your batteries.
- Take a good look at the world around you. Notice the little things like a bird in the sky, or an insect on the ground.
- Learn to appreciate the trees and flowers. Sometimes we rush everywhere in our cars and don't have time to notice that nature is all around us.
- Find time to talk to other people. After all, we are all going through the same processes. Learn to share your thoughts and others will share theirs with you. Be more tolerant of each other.
- Do kind things for other people around you. It does not need to involve money. You could smile at a complete stranger. You never know they may need it. Allow someone through a door before you step through it. Give up your

seat on a train. Just add your helping hand around, if only for a few moments.

- Concentrate on "today." Not tomorrow or next week, only the here and now.
- Expect setbacks then they won't knock you down unexpectedly. They will happen; pick yourself up, brush yourself down and move on.
- Talk to yourself when no one's around. You are your best listener.

Perhaps you already practice some of our suggestions above. Learning to cope with anxious moments means re-training how you think. Once conquered, it is a new lifestyle that should stay with you for good. Think more positive thoughts and your smile will come naturally. That's because you have put stress and anxiety at bay.

Conclusion

At the beginning of this book, I set out to show you how CBT can be a successful treatment for curing anxiety. Mental health issues imbalance your thoughts. It is my hope that by trying some of these methods, you can learn to reach deep within yourself. By doing this you will begin to make major changes to your life. Mental health imbalances are debilitating to everyday life. The important factor here is that they are curable.

When we think of an illness, often we assume the treatment to be pharmaceutical or surgery. Rarely do we stop and understand that the cure could be the power of our own mind. This is where some may accuse us of entering the realms of spiritual practice. Yet, scientific studies show that we can physically alter the processes in our body, by using our minds.

When threatened with danger, it is only natural that the brain alerts the rest of our body to take the necessary action. But, sometimes we perceive a danger that isn't actually there. When that happens, the body begins the process of protection. By learning to recognize the autonomous reactions in your own body, you can learn how to control them. That is how easy it can be. Taking control of those maladaptive thoughts will completely alter your hormonal output. This is not rocket science, but it is medical facts on how the human body works.

CBT is not only successful in treating psychological conditions but medical ones too. It is proven to help with pain. A study by Yu, Norton & McCracken (2017) using a new technique in CBT called Acceptance and Commitment Therapy (ACT) helps with pain management (conc.a). Further CBT can also be effective in helping those who suffer from Insomnia. (Wagley et.al. 2012) . (conc.b).

You will not notice changes overnight. It takes practice to force your thoughts to go in a different direction. It takes practice to get those meditational exercises to kick in as soon as your body hits the alert button. These methods are life-changing. Once established, they can become a permanent part of living an anxiety-free existence.

References

6b) Anxiety and Depression Association of America, (2013) Available at https://adaa.org/about-adaa/press-room/facts-statistics, accessed 10-12-2018.

1b) Chiang KJ, Tsai JC, Liu D, Lin CH, Chiu HL, Chou KR. Efficacy of cognitive-behavioral therapy in patients with bipolar disorder: A meta-analysis of randomized controlled trials {published online May 4, 2017]. PLoS One.doi:10.1371/journal.pone.0176849

1c) Beutel ME, Stark R, Pan H, et al. Changes of brain activation pre- post short-term psychodynamic inpatient psychotherapy: an fMRI study of panic disorder patients. Psychiatry Res. 2010;184:96-104

4.2b) Boelen, P. A., de Keijser, J., van den Hout, M. A., & van den Bout, J. (2007). 'Treatment of complicated grief: A comparison between cognitive-behavioral therapy and supportive counseling.' Journal of Consulting and Clinical Psychology, 75(2), pp 277-284.

4.4a) Brian C. Chu; Daniela Colognori; Adam S. Weissman; Katie Bannon (2009) 'An Initial Description and Pilot of Group Behavioral Activation Therapy for Anxious and Depressed Youth', Cognitive and Behavioral Practice, ISSN: 1077-7229, Vol: 16, Issue: 4, Page: 408-419

4.5c). Richard P. Brown and Patricia L. Gerbarg Sudarshan Kriya Yogic Breathing in the Treatment of Stress, Anxiety, and Depression: Part II—Clinical Applications and Guidelines The Journal of Alternative and Complementary Medicine 2005 11:4, 711-717

4.2a) Bryant, R. A., Moulds, M. L., Guthrie, R. M., Dang, S. T., & Nixon, R. D. V. (2003). 'Imaginal exposure alone and imaginal exposure with cognitive restructuring in treatment of posttraumatic stress disorder.' Journal of Consulting and Clinical Psychology, 71(4), 706-712.4.2b)

4.7b) Creswell C, Waite P, Cooper PJ (2014) Assessment and management of anxiety disorders in children and adolescentsArchives of Disease in Childhood 2014;99:674-678

6c) Gellatly, J., Bower, P., Hennessy, S., Richards, D., Gilbody, S., & Lovell, K. (2007). What makes self-help interventions effective in the management of depressive symptoms? Meta-analysis and meta-regression. Psychological Medicine, 37(9), 1217-1228. doi:10.1017/S0033291707000062

4.5a Goldin P. R., Gross J. J. (2010). Effects of mindfulness-based stress reduction (4.5a). (MBSR) on emotion regulation in social anxiety disorder. Emotion 10, 83–91. 10.1037/a0018441

1a) Grossman P, Niemann L, Schmidt S, Walach H. Mindfulness-based stress reduction and health benefits. A meta-analysis. J Psychosom Res. 2004;57(1):35-43

2c) Hackett RA, Kivimäki M, Kumari M, Steptoe A. Diurnal cortisol patterns, future diabetes, and impaired glucose metabolism in the Whitehall II Cohort Study. J Clin Endocrinol Metab. 2016;101(2):619-625.

6a) Harai, M. & Clum GA. (2006), 'A meta-analytic study of self-help interventions for anxiety problems' Behav Ther. 2006 Jun;37(2):99-111

4.7e) Khanna, SM, and Kendal PC (2010) Computer-Assisted Cognitive Behavioral Therapy for Child Anxiety: Results of a Randomized Clinical Trial,

Journal of Consulting and Clinical Psychology, 2010, Vol. 78, No. 5, 737–745

4.1a) Kirkham, A. J. Breeze J.M. Paloma, M.B. (2011) 'The impact of verbal instructions on goal-directed behaviour' Acta Psychologica Volume 139, Issue 1, January 2012, pp 212-219

4.7d) Minde K, Roy J, Bezonsky R, Hashemi A. The effectiveness of CBT in 3–7 year old anxious children: Preliminary data. J Can Acad Child Adolesc Psychiatry. 2010;19:109–15.

2a) McAuley MT, Kenny RA, Kirkwood TB, Wilkinson DJ, Jones JJ, Miller VM (March 2009). "A mathematical model of aging-related and cortisol induced hippocampal dysfunction". BMC Neuroscience. 10: 26. doi:10.1186/1471-2202-10-26. PMC 2680862. PMID 19320982.

4.7a) Muris, P. & Broeren, S (2008) 'Twenty-five Years of Research on Childhood Anxiety Disorders: Publication Trends Between 1982 and 2006 and a Selective Review of the Literature' J Child Fam Stud. 2009 Aug; 18(4): 388–395.

conc.a). Yu, L. Norton, S. & McCracken L.M. Change in "Self-as-Context" ("Perspective-Taking") Occurs in Acceptance and Commitment Therapy for People With Chronic Pain and Is Associated With Improved Functioning The Journal of Pain, Volume 18, Issue 6, 664 - 672

4.7c) Piacentini J, Roblek T. Recognizing and treating childhood anxiety disorders. West J Med. 2002;176:149–151. doi: 10.1136/ewjm.176.3.149.

2b) de Quervain DJ, Roozendaal B, McGaugh JL (August 1998). "Stress and glucocorticoids impair retrieval of long-term spatial memory". Nature. 394

(6695): 787–90. Bibcode:1998 Natur.394.787D.
doi:10.1038/29542. PMID 9723618

5a) Barbara Olasov Rothbaum and Ann C. Schwartz
Exposure Therapy for Posttraumatic Stress Disorder
American Journal of Psychotherapy 2002 56:1, 59-75

4.5b). Tang, Yi-Yuan & Holzel, Britta & Posner,
Michael. (2015). The neuroscience of mindfulness
meditation. Nature Reviews Neuroscience. 16.
10.1038/nrn3916.

4.7d) Turner SM, Beidel DC, Costello A.
Psychopathology in the offspring of anxiety disorder
patients. Journal of Consulting and Clinical
Psychology. 1987;55:229–235.

conc.b). Wagley, J. N., Rybarczyk, B., Nay, W. T.,
Danish, S. and Lund, H. G. (2013), Effectiveness of
Abbreviated CBT for Insomnia in Psychiatric

Outpatients: Sleep and Depression Outcomes. J. Clin. Psychol., 69: 1043-1055.

5b) Jaye Wald & Steven Taylor (2005) 'Interoceptive Exposure Therapy Combined with Trauma-related Exposure Therapy for Post-traumatic Stress Disorder: a Case Report,' Cognitive Behaviour Therapy 34:1, 34-40

Disclaimer

The information contained in **"Cognitive Behavioral Therapy For Anxiety"** and its components, is meant to serve as a comprehensive collection of strategies that the author of this eBook has done research about. Summaries, strategies, tips and tricks are only recommendations by the author, and reading this eBook will not guarantee that one's results will exactly mirror the author's results.

The author of this Ebook has made all reasonable efforts to provide current and accurate information for the readers of this eBook. The author and its associates will not be held liable for any unintentional errors or omissions that may be found.

The material in the Ebook may include information by third parties. Third party materials comprise of opinions expressed by their owners. As such, the

147

author of this eBook does not assume responsibility or liability for any third party material or opinions.

The publication of third party material does not constitute the author's guarantee of any information, products, services, or opinions contained within third party material. Use of third party material does not guarantee that your results will mirror our results. Publication of such third party material is simply a recommendation and expression of the author's own opinion of that material.

Whether because of the progression of the Internet, or the unforeseen changes in company policy and editorial submission guidelines, what is stated as fact at the time of this writing may become outdated or inapplicable later.

whole or in parts. No parts of this report may be reproduced or retransmitted in any forms whatsoever without the written expressed and signed permission from the author.

Made in the USA
Las Vegas, NV
21 May 2024

90202232R00088